Your
Simple Guide
To Creating

Mission, Vision & Value Statements

By Stuart Rice

Stuart Rice
"The Simple Guide to Creating Your Mission, Vision & Value Statements"
©2020, Stuart Rice
Self-published
(stuart.rice@levelupyoursales.com)

First Edition

Dedicated to Mary

Table of Contents

Introduction

I remember the first time I was introduced to the importance of a Mission statement. I was trying to secure funding for a company I was starting, and one of the requirements was a Mission statement. I paused.

I didn't know what a Mission statement was, or why they would need it. I did know that I needed money, so I figured that I would have to write one, so I did the one thing I know how to do really well: I Googled it.

Sifting through all of the different suggestions and templates and even paying for books and online resources, I came to the conclusion that I was not going to be able to come up with a compelling statement, because I couldn't figure out what it was that I was trying to say.

Eventually, I figured it out, wrote up the proposal that I needed to finish, and turned it in. I got the funding. I moved on with my life. I can't even remember what the Mission statement for that company was. It wasn't important to me, it was just an obstacle.

When I decided to start this company, I was faced with a similar challenge. But this time something was different. I was smarter, more savvy, and now understood why a mission statement is so important: it establishes who you are. Without it, it becomes increasingly difficult to navigate what you do with other people. You start to get lost, and that is exactly what happened with that company.

Developing these statements will help you and your company. Whether you are just trying to get funding or establish a company culture, these statements will make it easy to convey your message and cut down on any confusion, both externally with your customers and internally with your employees.

The book is designed so that you can uncover these answers for yourself, so no need to endlessly search for resources, you will be able to come up with great Mission / Vision / Value statements that feel important to you, and you will remember them. You will also live them, which is what all successful companies do.

I am excited for you to uncover your statements and look forward to hearing about your successful implementation!

About the Author

Stuart Rice has spent the last 25 years working in sales so that he could write this book and help others discover their own success stories through his company, Level Up.

From selling music in a mall store to growing enterprise sales by 500%, Stuart has gained experience from both the buying and selling perspective for both B2B and B2C. Now, he wants to help you enjoy working with people as much as he has.

When not writing or coaching, Stuart enjoys speaking with interesting people on his podcast "Sketch Comedy Podcast Show." He also enjoys spending time with his children, who are all too big to sit on his lap. He splits his time between Portland, OR and Denver, CO where his lovely partner lives.

How to Use This Book

Purchasing the book was great, and I appreciate it because I still have kids to feed. My goal is for you, and the only way to do that is by doing the work in the workbook.

When it is time to write, do not worry about spelling, punctuation, grammar, or how it looks. Focus on getting your words and ideas on the page, you can clean it up later. The magic of writing is that it does some exciting things to your brain, like continuing to process subconsciously, which helps the information attach to your neurons. This book, for example, went through three rewrites. THREE! It's practically a part of me now.

Please write in the sidebar, highlight, doodle, whatever you would like to the pages of this book, it is yours, and I thank you for making the purchase!

The sections of the book are set up like this:

1. An introduction to the concept.

2. Some exercises to help you with perception and understanding. Instructions will always be *bold italicized* for you.

3. Real-World tool development that you can implement into your business immediately.

4. A recap and little quiz to help solidify the knowledge you just gained.

Here is how to use this book:

1. When you see *Instructions*, just go ahead and write in the space provided below

2. Find a place that makes it comfortable and easy to work without getting sleepy. Group settings or working with someone else is best.

3. Be prepared to take a break if you start to get drowsy.

4. This book is not sacred, highlight and note like crazy.

5. Have fun.

Some things to know:

1. Throughout the book I refer to "customers" as the people you will be working with. Sometimes I used "customers or clients" or "clients". They are all the same thing, Customers are usually transactional, clients are usually relational and in this book they are treated one-in-the-same.

2. I have taken a very causal tone in the book, not to be too relaxed but because of the amount of time involved in going through this book. It's a long haul, and having a bit of levity is good.

3. There are other ways to go through the course. If you are finding that you have a hard time doing it on your own, visit **levelupyoursales.com** to see options that will make the course easier and more collaborative.

Get ready to change your perception of what you do and get excited to work with customers again or, for some of you, for the very first time!

Additional Resources

Level Up offers quick courses for all available books at amazingly low prices.

Visit levelupyoursales.com for more information, schedules, and links to sign up for hands-on workshops.

Additionally, get a FREE PDF of the worksheets for this book if you sign up for the weekly newsletter. Do that at levelupyoursales.com/subscribe

This book is available as an audiobook from Audible, where you can get this title for free as well as over 300,000 others. Do that by going to https://levelupyoursales.com/book

Knowing Yourself

"Knowing yourself is the beginning of all wisdom."

- Aristotle

The first thing we need to do is create a clear definition of you.

When you picture yourself, what do you see? How do other people perceive you? How do you want other people to see you?

Being authentic is not overrated. When you are authentic, it is impossible to lie, which means you are trustworthy. Authenticity is grounding, and when you are talking to someone who is grounded, the conversation feels comfortable and safe. Unfortunately, people mistake authenticity for eccentricity and give themselves permission for erratic and poor behavior.

Understand that being late all of the time is eccentric, it is a strange and inconsiderate behavior to have towards others. Stating that you are not timely does not make it authentic, it becomes an excuse. If you are late because of traffic, be honest about it and willfully try to be at the next meeting on time, that is authentic. If you are late because you are "always 15 minutes late," then you are eccentric. Eccentric behavior makes other people feel incredibly uncomfortable, not a trait we want to show our customers.

Our goal is to be authentic, to find deep within ourselves how we want to project ourselves, and take steps to fulfill that image.

It starts with our own words about ourselves. Words are tricky, and often abandon us at the worst possible times. We can avoid this loss of words by creating descriptions of ourselves that illustrate how we want to be seen and committing to using these words consistently when we talk to people. Words are like magic, and if we use these words often enough, we can conjure our intent into reality.

In this section, we are going to answer three fundamental questions about you:

What do you do?

Where do you want to go?

How do you conduct yourself?

Creating the answers to these questions will: clarify what people can expect from you, tell them what you are trying to accomplish, and how they can expect to be treated by you or your company.

Whether you are talking to a consumer or a top-level decision-maker, this information helps that person understand who you are. This understanding builds bonds of trust.

Let's start with a fun little exercise that will get us to begin interestingly thinking about yourself. A little inside perspective/outside perspective on who you are.

Write down the first 5 words that you would associate with yourself.

Don't think, just write:

Were the words different? That's okay! We will be working with all of these words to build a vision of you that works for all.

These words represent your ideal, authentic self. Wherever the words have come from, these are the ones that mean the most to you and are the ones we will focus on to define you. If you feel they are currently not authentic, but you have the desire to make them authentic, we will create tools later on that will help you achieve that goal.

Did you already have a statement you were ready with? If not, you will, I promise.

How would you say others describe what you do?

As in the previous exercise, what would you like to do? Be aspirational.

That one is difficult. What I want to be doing is napping. When I think of what I want to do with my work life I tend to limit my own potential, telling myself that my ideal vision of my career is too lofty. Limits are good for speeds on the freeway or blood alcohol levels before driving, but are terrible for realizing our potential and striving for our dreams.

On the next page is a list of words. Do not be intimidated, there is no spelling test.

Sustainability / Innovation / Excellence / Reliability / Loyal /

Committed / Dependable / Passionate / Courageous /

Respectful / Inspiring / Honesty / Integrity / Consistent /

Efficient / Humorous / Optimistic / Positive / Nurturing /

Open-minded / Adventurous / Resourceful /

Customer Service / Fun / Humble / Community /

Responsibility / Quality / Satisfaction / Delight / Support /

Caring / Partnership / Best / Value / Global / Transformation /

Leadership / Teamwork / Diversity / Humility / Transparency /

Results / Fanatical / Friends / Family / Listening / Learning /

Educating / Remarkable

Highlighting is fun, isn't it? A nice break from having to write things down. Be aware, we have more writing to do.

Mission / Vision / Values Statements

The most successful companies in the world all have Mission, Vision, and Value statements. Not because these statements look good in a business plan or on a plaque on the wall, but successful companies create them because they work.

Why these three statements are so vital to a company's success:

- **A Mission Statement** defines who you are and what you do.
- **A Vision Statement** outlines where you want to go and creates direction.
- **A Values Statement** informs others about your principals and what people can expect.

These three statements answer the questions that we asked before the exercises, and now we are going to craft them into useable statements just for you.

"For what purpose?" You might ask.

Could you imagine going on a date and asking, "Hello, what is your name?" and getting a shrug in response? Asking "What would you like to do tonight?" only to receive a blank stare? Asking them to "Tell me about yourself." with the only response being a head scratch and a yawn? How exciting does this date sound? It seems like a good time to ask for the check, but not in a good way.

Imagine meeting with a prospective client, and they ask you, "What is it that you do?" Without a decent answer, they are going to look at you, much like you would look at your silent date.

You might think, "A name and a question about what I do are not the same thing." You're right, knowing what you do is FAR more important. Think about watching movies with your parents or other elders, how often do they see someone and blurt out "that's the guy from…" but they can't remember what the actor's name is? They do not remember the name, but they recall the actor's body of work. That is why establishing what you do is so important.

Recognition of you and what you do builds trust in your ability, even without proof. Without trust, people will question everything that you say. You can continually build trust by getting people to remember your name AND what it is you do.

We will use the information from the section before and give you something better than a name, and we are going to give you a purpose.

Let's start with the Mission Statement, then create our Vision Statement, then develop our Values Statement.

Mission Statement | What You Do

"What do you do?"

"I sell stuff."

Inspiring words. I know when I ask someone what they do for a living, and that is their response, I suddenly get very excited to talk more in-depth with them. Keep in mind that I am trying to get a coaching customer. That answer is too vague with too many unknowns. It sounds like they sell drugs or hemorrhoid cream; it feels like they are hiding something.

Before you scoff, how do you tell people what it is that you do? The last time someone asked, what did you say you did for a living? Be honest about what you said.

Write down your response the last time someone asked what you do:

Looking at your response above, does it define who you are? Does it clearly explain what you do? Read your words out loud; does it reveal to someone why you are special?

We are all guilty of the "I sell stuff" type of response. We get bashful or feel like it isn't the appropriate time. It might be you have not thought about how to respond to this question, and that was the simplest response.

A well-crafted mission statement defines who you are, what you do, and why you are unique. The statement will be your guide on how you present yourself to other people and how other people will perceive you. Making a compelling mission statement is pretty essential.

Success-minded businesses all have a mission statement. Start there: does your current business have an established mission statement?

Write your company's current mission statement (if none, leave blank):

Let's review the statement: How do you feel when you read it? Does it feel natural? Do you do an action daily to help make that statement a reality? Hopefully, the answer is yes because that is what a mission statement is for: an inspirational guiding light for the organization to follow.

Did you find yourself realizing your company does not have a mission statement, or that you did not know of one? Do you know there is a mission statement, and you can't remember it? That's okay. We are going to give you the tools to craft your own.

Your company is not the only company that you admire. Let's take a look at their Mission statements!

Company 1

Company 2

Company 3

Is there one above that spoke to you? One that you feel defines what the company does? Put a star next to it.

When written well, a mission statement is interchangeable with the name of the company.

Find someone, maybe even phone a friend you haven't talk to in a while, and ask them to play a game with you: give them the mission statement and see if they can figure out what company it is.

A fun game, let's play a round of that here. Base it off of the statement, see if you can guess which company it is by only their mission statement.

Guess the Mission Statements!

"To be one of the world's leading producers and providers of
entertainment and information, using its portfolio of brands to
differentiate its content, services and consumer products."

Company

"Bring inspiration and innovation to every athlete in the world.
If you have a body, you are an athlete."

Company

"To be Earth's most customer-centric company,
where customers can find and discover anything they might want to buy
online,
and endeavors to offer its customers the lowest possible prices."

Company

That's fun! Were you able to guess which companies had which Mission
Statements? Did some sound pretty similar? Again, when done correctly,
the Mission Statement has more meaning and gives a company a better
definition than most of the marketing and advertising they do. More

importantly, these statements are in their marketing and advertising, and you didn't realize it!

Now that you have seen some examples of excellent mission statements, we want to start working on creating that for you and your company.

What does your company do for people?

Who does your company want to do that for?

What sets you apart from other companies or people that do the same thing?

We have seen some examples, we have written down some notes about your company, let's try to craft a mission statement and see how we do:

Let's share that with the group. If not with a group, read it out loud. Sounds silly, but when you read it out-loud vs. just reading it on paper, you can hear if it makes sense or not.

Remember those words that you wrote down before? The five that you came up with on Page 20? Guess what we are going to do with those?

Write down your written words from the "Knowing Yourself" section.

Rewrite your Mission Statement above and try to use all 5 words above.

Read that one out loud. Better? When you read that statement, does it feel like you have defined what it is that you do? If people saw it on your website, or you said it in conversation, would they have a pretty good idea of what you would be able to do for them?

One of the beautiful things about doing this in a group is that you get feedback. Feedback is the sound that you get from your improperly set up guitar or microphone, and lets you know that it is time to reconfigure. Feedback is also what you receive from people when you need to make a change. Less annoying loud sounds, but can be just as irritating to our ears. Be accepting of feedback. It is genuinely going to help you set up your equipment or set up your business in the right way. If you are interested in getting immediate feedback from like-minded and motivated people, head to levelupyoursales.com and look into joining a team coaching session.

How do you feel about the mission statement you just wrote?

Without looking back, try writing it again.

Were you able to remember it? If so, it's probably a pretty good mission statement!

As you continue in the book, you might realize that you want to add more or trim parts of this statement, and that is perfect. This statement should feel awesome and give you chills when you think about what it means for you and your company, so if a change is required, please make that change.

Now, when people ask you what you do, you have a great place to start that conversation. The words may not come out as written; if you follow the sentiment and become consistent in using these words, you will find it is enlightening in conversation. Great job!

Vision Statement | Where You Want To Go

With a Mission Statement, we establish what we do right now. Designed to be present and to take the guesswork out of defining what it is that you do.

What about tomorrow? Or next week? Or five years from now?

Next on the list is deciding what you want your company to do in the future. Where do you want your company to be? How big? How successful? Start to manifest that ideal: with your vision statement. Working and doing the tasks connected to your Mission Statement should also be helping you progress and achieve your vision statement.

Vision statements are tricky, they cannot be too lofty, and they cannot be too small. I suggest a 12-month vision statement to start: where do you want your business to be 12 months from today? If you have an established business, what is the ultimate goal of your company? Market domination? State domination? National domination? World domination? Galaxy domination? You get to choose!

The difference between a mission and a vision statement is outward versus inward. Mission statements are outward and public, vision statements are inward, driving you and your company, and not always shared. Everyone in the organization needs to know the vision statement, but not everyone outside of the organization.

Formatting a vision statement can be surprisingly vague. It boils down to what allows you and your organization to conceptualize where it is you want to be.

Continue to consider making this vision statement for the next 12 months.

Who are the people you are hoping to help? What business are they in, or what is it they are trying to achieve? For example, entrepreneurs who are seeing growth in their business. No need to be overly specific.

Whose lives are you trying to improve?

Later we will be talking about this customer in-depth and discovering a lot of information about them. Still, right now, we want to identify them, so we can learn to visualize what their lives look like before working with us or buying our product, and after.

What is the primary goal of your company? When you are acquiring the above customers, what is your vision of success with them? You can create goals focused on revenue, but they can also be on customer satisfaction, diversification, growth, savings, or any other measurable.

Think about the primary goal in your business for this customer, what is it?

After looking at your goal, do you feel that the world will be a better place? I hope so because I am rooting for you. Make sure that it is positive and a trait that people will want. If your goal is to receive the fewest bad reviews, for instance, you might want to rephrase it to get the most positive reviews.

Who else does what you do? It is pretty rare to be the only company or individual in a particular industry, so consider all of the other people and organizations that do what you do. Are there some that are bigger? Is there one you admire? How will you compete with them on the above goal over the next 12 months?

Compared to your competition, where do you want your customers to rank you?

Do you want to be #1? Great! Are you okay with being #2? It might be time to rethink your position. Here is the argument for being #1: #1 survives. When things such as recessions, industry changes, and other hardships arise, #1 thrives. So, whatever market you are going after, be #1 in that market. Be the top dog. Be the queen bee. Be whatever animal you want, just be the best.

Vision statements are more difficult to find than mission statements. Take the company you admired from the previous chapter and try to look up their vision statement.

Write down a company that you admire and their Vision statement.

Is that a pretty good goal? Do you believe that they achieve those goals? Do they do that for you?

Look at top businesses, one of the things you will notice is that they do not strive to be #1, they already are #1. Our vision should be aspirational, so even if we achieve the top spot in our industry, we still have a reason to grow. Amazon is the top company in their field, thus making the statement that they want to be #1 is entirely benign. Instead, having a vision of 100% customer satisfaction is where they should aspire.

Can a Vision Statement change? Absolutely, and it should. Remember, this is our internal reminder of what we want to accomplish; if our goals change or our priorities change, we need to change the Vision Statement as well. Vision statements are pragmatic. However, they should never reflect a decrease in business. It is better to keep a lofty vision that is harder to attain than one that surrenders to failure.

Let's try to write our first vision statement:

How was that? Try saying out loud and see how it feels. Do you have someone close-by that you experiment with? Your audience does not have to be a business expert, but they should be able to figure out what you want to do going forward based on the statement you say to them.

Remember the 5 words you circled on page 20? Would any of those be applicable here?:

Adding some or all of these words to your vision reinforces their importance.

Your vision statement should give you goosebumps when you think about attaining it. Where you are going to journey over the next 12 months, think about what that would mean for your life, to see yourself in that situation. Does it have an impact on your financial health, your status in your community, self-worth?

A purpose is such a motivator.

Now, rewrite your vision statement.
Add the words, but try your best to produce it from memory:

What do you think? Is that a goal you would feel great about achieving? Can you see yourself doing something every day to help get you there?

Vision statements are great to look at every day. Make a poster. Put it on a Post-It note on your computer or refrigerator. Write it in lipstick on every bathroom mirror you see, unless you are at my house. Make your Vision Statement visible so that it becomes part of your day and can serve to remind you of your full potential.

Visualizing yourself achieving this goal will make it more exciting to do the mundane things every day.

Values Statement | How You Conduct Yourself

Company culture. Often, this is the top reason, right behind having a lousy boss, people leave a company. Not money. Not work/life balance. The biggest reason is how they feel the company views them; in an under-appreciated and untrustworthy way.

It is also the reason that a lot of owners get so frustrated with their employees.

"My company would never [insert awful thing here]. I would never tolerate it!"

The owner would not, but their untrained and unknowing employee might.

Company culture issues can stem from a lack of a values statement or, worse, ignoring or not knowing the values statement.

Value statements are simply the code of conduct for a company. This statement can be a list of words that help define the expectations of the treatment of employees and customers.

"But it's only me, I don't need to tell myself, do I?"

Yes, you do. Stress can cause people to do and say things they regret later and, unless you work for a beanbag company as a nap tester, stress is going to be a factor. When crafted appropriately, a vision statement will help keep you on track and serve as a promise to yourself, your organization, and your customers of how you define professionalism.

One of my favorite Values Statements was Google's original: "Don't do evil." Simple, concise, effective, and easy to ignore.

Good? Concise? Clear? Do you have a good sense of how they make decisions after reading this?

Remember that list of words on page 25? Go back and look at the words you circled. Do these words help define an ethical Values Statement? Are there words you would like to add?

Pick at least 5, but not more than 8, words that really describe your values from the highlighted words in the "Knowing Yourself" section.

The Vision Statement will help guide anyone in your organization when they need to make a decision. You can simply just list the words above and call it a day, but I think it is beneficial to add some definition.

Define how you expect the treatment of your customers, how your employees treat each other, and a guideline for expectations in decision making. That should cover most of your bases.

To make sure we are making the best choices on words, write down why you have picked those words.

Word 1

Word 2

Word 3

Word 4

Word 5

Word 6

Understanding the meaning behind these words gives them substance and something you can use to convey to others. The beautiful part about creating a vision statement is that there is no need to be eloquent or loquacious. A concise list of words with an understanding of their meaning behind them works just fine.

Write your vision statement!

With this statement, you can now keep yourself and others in-check with their words and actions. At any time, you can observe the behavior and ask, "Is this a good representation of [pick a word from your vision statement]." If it is not, then it is time to change that behavior. Keeping it simple allows for anyone to know if they are operating within the boundaries of appropriate action, internally and externally, of the company.

You just completed three crucial, personal, and very difficult-to-compose statements for yourself. If you do not feel a sense of pride, you are a better person than I am; you have earned the right to puff out your chest and feel accomplished.

On the next page, you are going to commit these three statements to paper again, all together, and ready for posting somewhere you can see it. Own these statements, they are yours, and they define your business and you as an individual with a purpose.

Your Mission / Vision / Values Statements

Mission Statement - What You Do

Repeat your Mission Statement:

Vision Statement - Where You Are Going

Repeat your Vision Statement.

Values Statement - How You Are Doing It

Repeat your Values Statement.

Now that you have these established and know what you do, how you do it and where you are going to go with it, we can start working on the rest of the tools that will help establish you as a bonafide badass and why people are going to want to work with you, or at least seek advice from you.

Mission / Vision / Values Takeaways

These three statements help discover and define your business.

- A Mission Statement defines who you are, what you do, who you do it for and what makes you unique.

- A Vision Statement outlines where you would like to take your business.

- A Values Statement establishes your expectation of behavior, for both yourself and your employees, and how customers can expect to be treated.

Quiz

1. **Mission statements…**

    1. …are handed out to employees with instructions on how to accomplish a goal.

    2. …are designed to outline the expectations of conduct in a company.

    3. …define what you do.

2. **Vision statements should be shared with everyone.**

    1. True

    2. False

3. **Where is a value statement best displayed?**

    1. Visible to all employees and customers.

    2. In the bathroom.

    3. Tattoo'd on your chest and stomach.

    4. The employee break room.

Conclusion

How do you feel after completing that? Pretty good? You should. There are a lot of small businesses, and even some larger businesses, that do not have these statements.

I suggest learning them, tweaking them, and really start implementing them into your life. When you have distinct and clear rules, it makes decision-making, training, and interactions with others much easier and more fun!

Interested in More?

Level Up offers quick courses for all of the available books at amazingly low prices.

Visit levelupyoursales.com for more information, schedules, and links to sign up for hands-on workshops.

Additionally, get a FREE PDF of the worksheets for this book if you sign up for the weekly newsletter. Do that at levelupyoursales.com/subscribe

This book is available as an audiobook from Audible, where you can get this title for free as well as over 300,000 others. Do that by going to https://levelupyoursales.com/book